495

The Art Institute of Chicago: The Stock Exchange Trading Room

THE ART INSTITUTE OF CHICAGO: THE STOCK EXCHANGE TRADING ROOM

by John Vinci
Vinci-Kenny, Architects
Stock Exchange Trading Room Reconstruction

The Art Institute of Chicago

The research for this volume has been made possible through the generosity of the Walter E. Heller Foundation.

Designed by Harvey Retzloff
Composition by Frederic Ryder Company
Printed in the United States of America
by Congress Printing Company

CONTENTS

Credits

PHOTOGRAPHS: Hedrich-Blessing, cover, 47, 54, 55, 58, 59; Michael J. Pado, 2, 44, 48, 56, 57; J. W. Taylor, 11, 27; Richard Nickel, 12, 13, 14, 15, 16, 22, 23, 28, 29, 31, 37, 38, 41, 42, 43; *Architectural Record*, Great American Architects Series, No. 2 (December 1895), 19; *Ornamental Iron*, II (July 1894), 20; *History of Chicago*, Chicago Interocean (1900), 24; John Vinci, 45, 46, 50, 52; The Art Institute of Chicago, 60.

ILLUSTRATIONS: Courtesy of Avery Library, Columbia University, 21, 30, 32, 33; Vinci-Kenny, Architects, 25, 26, 49, 51, 53; Crombie Taylor Associates, 34, 35.

Richard Nickel 1928–1972

Most of the photographs of the Chicago Stock Exchange Building in this study are the work of Richard Nickel. A graduate of the Institute of Design, Illinois Institute of Technology in 1954, Nickel went on to receive a Master of Photography degree three years later. Nickel's master's thesis, *A Photographic Documentation of Adler and Sullivan*, resulted in the discovery of many projects by the firm which were previously unknown.

When the opportunity came to work on dismantling the Trading Room for the Art Institute, he agreed to join the effort and make the necessary photographs.

On January 31, 1972, the salvaging of the Trading Room was completed. On April 13, 1972, Nickel went into the partially wrecked building and was not seen again. His body was found four weeks later in the débris.

PREFACE

The Trading Room of The Chicago Stock Exchange
may well be the most celebrated interior of the First
Chicago School of Architecture. It can surely be
called the most successful interior of its time created
in the United States. It was designed for a special
purpose: trading; this required freedom of movement
and the requirements of a huge volume of space, combined with enough intimacy to make the human voice
readily heard without modern amplification. As no
one today was present to eavesdrop when Adler &
Sullivan were planning the room itself speculation
only permits one to guess whose share was which.
For acoustical reasons, one may suspect that Adler
worked out the details of the forms and spaces, al-
ways, of course, with the consent and advice of his
inspired colleague. On the other hand, one may rea-
sonably be sure that Sullivan planned the ornamentation and, above all, the exquisitely rich scheme of
color. His use of stenciled designs on the walls have
reminded some observers of the Book of Kells, but
these same observers forget that William Butterfield,
two generations earlier, as well as many others, used
comparable and personal systems of flat wall decoration (usually in tile). Sullivan's personal idiosyncrasy
was to avoid, in large measure, references to the past,
though, of course, his work is full of it. Even the four
great piers in the Trading Room recall pages from
Viollet-le-Duc, and the panelling of mahogany is rea-
sonably straightforward Georgian survival, just as
the use of gilding and scagliola on the piers has
equally good 18th-century precedent. (Granted that

the precedents do not *look* like Sullivan's work, they are there and they explain Sullivan's thought.)

For each of Sullivan's (or Adler's) distinctive usages there are precedents: Chester Cheston used stained glass skylights in S. Mark's, Dalston, London, before 1870, of which it is improbable that either of the Chicago architects knew, but it is neither precedents of the immediate nor the ancient past which are of importance in comprehending their work, most especially in this noble interior. What is of supreme importance is how the elements used were conceived and blended together to achieve a noble space equalled in the United States in the nineteenth century only by Latrobe's original interior for the Assumption, Baltimore. Indeed, it is true that there is more than enough in the interior of the Stock Exchange Room to make it both novel and individual, but, it is not novelty which makes for distinction; it is how the elements are disposed and how they are adjusted to their function which makes for their distinction, and the perfection and subtlety of details. (After all, there was not that much about Hagia Sophia without precedent, and the Parthenon is the summation and perfection of a tradition.) The Stock Exchange Room expresses the elegance of its form and concept and the way in which both were apposite for the purpose for which the room was put. The use of the restored room, as a concourse and a gathering place, the drawing room of The Art Institute of Chicago (if one will), is not unlike its original use as a gathering place for trading.

The arch of the Stock Exchange has been erected as a separate feature in the East Garden at Monroe Street and Columbus Drive. While it is out of anything resembling its original context, it is a handsome object and preserves one of the great elements of exterior architecture by Adler and Sullivan, and shows more readily the monumental side of the firm's work, for the Auditorium is hard to see.

The Art Institute of Chicago and the people of the country are immeasurably in the debt of the Walter E. Heller Foundation, and the imaginative generosity of its President, Mrs. Edwin J. DeCosta, who is unique, among Benefactors, in making those she helps feel they are granting *her* a favor, and who has made others' dreams come true: the room has been saved and replaced once more to be the grandest interior in the entire Middle West, and the arch is now a great triumphal entry for the East Garden, opened and dedicated for Chicago on April 6, 1977.

JOHN MAXON

8

ACKNOWLEDGMENTS

The reconstruction of Adler & Sullivan's Trading Room seemed inconceivable in the midst of demolition of the Chicago Stock Exchange Building in 1972. Yet even as the architectural fragments from the room were being dismantled and crated for removal to The Art Institute of Chicago, the museum enthusiastically began to support the effort. The Art Institute's staff recognized the architectural significance of the room, and promoted its reconstruction as a significant part of the building project to celebrate the museum's Centennial in 1979.

Through the generosity of the Walter E. Heller Foundation and its President, Mrs. Edwin J. DeCosta, the Trading Room and the entrance arch grew from a group of architectural fragments to a magnificent reconstructed room and archway. With the cooperation of Skidmore, Owings & Merrill, the Art Institute staff, and the Reed Illinois Corporation, the reconstruction was smoothly co-ordinated. Superior craftsmanship by all trades brought our drawings to realization.

Research was crucial to insure an accurate reconstruction by restoring features long absent. In this respect, the material assembled by Timothy Samuelson proved to be invaluable; Irma Strauss furnished us with new information on Sullivan's stencils.

Finally, the editorial help of David Norris, and the assistance of Kathleen Roy, made this record available to supplement the experience of seeing the Trading Room once again.

VINCI-KENNY, ARCHITECTS

INTRODUCTION

The Chicago Stock Exchange Building, designed in 1893 by the firm of Adler & Sullivan, stood, until its demolition in 1972, as a major contribution to the Chicago school of architecture. The building's richly ornamented second-floor Trading Room, which housed the activities of the Exchange, is now reconstructed as a public space in the east wing of The Art Institute of Chicago.

In 1960, the original Commission on Chicago Architectural Landmarks designated the Chicago Stock Exchange Building an official landmark. Since this Commission's ability to legally protect buildings was limited, a new Commission on Chicago Historical and Architectural Landmarks vested with broader powers, was established. The new Commission offered landmark designation to the property owners, who rejected it. The announcement by the owners to replace the building resulted in protest. Again the Commission, encouraged by preservation groups, voted in favor of designation. In order for landmark status to be granted to the Chicago Stock Exchange Building, the Commission's designation had to be approved by the City Council. If the city supported the designation, they would have had to buy or subsidize the building. After public hearings, the City Council voted against landmark designation for the Stock Exchange Building.

After it was clear that attempts to save the entire structure were futile, the City of Chicago negotiated with the corporate owners of the property, the developers, and the wrecking company to have a photographic documentation of the building made, and to acquire its major artifacts. Among these were the entrance arch, sections of the cornice, and the ornament of the Trading Room.

The Art Institute of Chicago, which was offered the first choice from the artifacts, decided that, in place of miscellaneous fragments, it would be more rewarding to request the ornament from the Trading Room. The Art Institute's Trustees assigned funds for the purpose of saving the room's stencils and plaster ornaments, in addition to material given by the Three Oaks Wrecking Company. From the generous gifts of Mrs. Eugene Davidson and the Graham Foundation for Advanced Studies in the Fine Arts, the Art Institute was able to buy additional elements. The architectural firm of Vinci-Kenny, which had participated in the removal of the artifacts, was consulted on the feasibility of rebuilding the whole room, and the project was launched. The reconstructed Trading Room was reopened in 1977.

Soon after the announcement of the Art Institute's Centennial Project, which was to include the construction of the wing housing the Trading Room, the City of Chicago generously offered the museum the Stock Exchange entrance archway. It has been reassembled at Monroe Street and Columbus Drive, adjacent to the new wing.

The Stock Exchange Building nearing completion in 1894.

Detail above the entrance arch of the building.

Detail of the arcade at the second and third floors of the building.

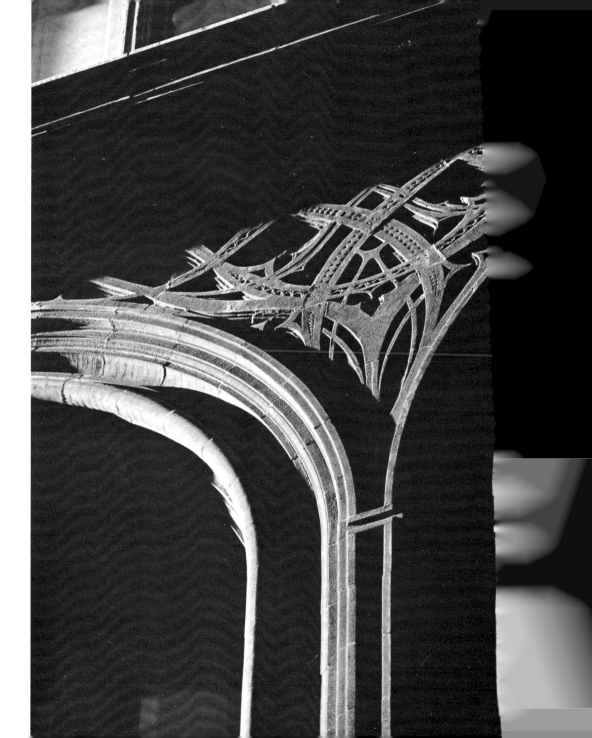

Detail of the cornice and the upper
floors of the building.

Detail of the LaSalle Street entrance
arch of the building showing the north
medallion specifying the date 1893, the
year construction began.

Detail of the LaSalle Street entrance arch of the building showing the south medallion depicting the Peck residence.

For nearly 80 years the Chicago Stock Exchange Building stood at the southwest corner of LaSalle and Washington Streets. Its light buff-colored terra-cotta façade seemed to loom forward and upward where LaSalle Street narrowed to the south.

The corner had been the homesite of the Philip Peck family. In the 1880s Ferdinand W. Peck, a son of the original settler, was to become a major client of Adler & Sullivan. From him came the commission for the temporary opera festival theater, built within the lakefront Exposition Building which stood where the Art Institute now is. This theater's success led to the commission for the Auditorium Building, a combination hotel, theater, and office building at Michigan Avenue and Congress Street, a building which brought Adler & Sullivan national fame.

The commission from Peck for the site at Washington and LaSalle Street stipulated a thirteen-story office building. It was decided to incorporate a major space into the structure for use as a trading room by the growing Chicago Stock Exchange, and, thus, to encourage office tenancy by brokerage firms and related professions. The Exchange was given a 15-year, rent-free lease and the building took its name.

The design of the building revealed Sullivan's famed dictum "Form follows Function." He codified this idea in his essay *The Tall Office Building Artistically Considered:*

Beginning with the first story, we give this a main entrance that attracts the eye to its location, and the remainder of the story we treat in a more or less liberal, expansive, sumptuous way—a way based exactly on the practical necessities, but expressed with a sentiment of largeness and freedom. The second story we treat in a similar way, but usually with milder pretension. Above this, throughout the indefinite number of typical office tiers, we take our cue from the individual cell, which requires a window with its separating pier, its sill and lintel, and we, without more ado, make them look all alike because they are all alike. This brings us to the attic, which, having no division into office-cells, and no special requirement for lighting, gives us the power to show by means of its broad expanse of wall, and its dominating weight and character, that which is the fact,—namely that the series of office tiers has come definitely to an end.

Although Sullivan wrote this essay in 1896, these principles, slightly modified, were used in the Chicago Stock Exchange Building. The great terra-cotta arch called attention to the entrance, and the remainder of the ground floor, occupied by shops, was treated straightforwardly. The second floor façade was not handled in a similar way, but combined with that of the third floor into a richly ornamented arcade, to reflect the presence of the Trading Room and an adjacent banking space. The typical office tiers were given variation by alternating "Chicago windows" with three-sided projecting bays. The attic story, concealed by an ornamental cornice, brought the building to a dramatic conclusion.

Construction, begun in the summer of 1893, was completed the following spring. Caisson foundations were designed by bridge engineer William Sooy Smith to support the west wall. This first use of such foundations in Chicago avoided the damage which might have occurred to newspaper presses in the adjacent

Herald Building had traditional pilings been driven in the area. Although the original cost of the building was estimated at $1,800,000, the financial panic of 1893 allowed bids to come in lower. Construction was slowed by strikes and interrupted by delays in receiving materials, but the final cost amounted to $1,131,555.

At the LaSalle Street entrance to the building, the architects elected to design a large terra-cotta portal, three bays wide and two stories high (approximately 40 by 30 feet), framing a semi-circular arch. This design element had been used in other Adler & Sullivan projects; the most prominent was the entrance to their Transportation Building for the World's Columbian Exposition in 1893. This "Golden Portal," a great steel-framed arch covered in a gilded plaster, was one of the most admired features of the Fair.

In the Stock Exchange Building, the portal and its arch served two functions. Attention was called to the main entrance, and the articulation of the arch's tympanum suggested that the ground floor and second floor were functionally inter-related. At the street level, vertical divisions provided for four double doors with ornamented bronze kickplates and hardware. An arched transom expressed the vaulted ceiling of the entrance vestibule, and the bronze lintel above defined the level of the second or main floor. The terra-cotta ornament for this entrance portal has been considered among Sullivan's most brilliant designs. Incorporated in the upper span-

Photograph taken of the LaSalle Street entrance arch before it was discovered that the Peck residence was not the first brick building in Chicago.

drels of the arch are two commemorative medallions, four feet in diameter. The left medallion depicts the house of Philip Peck, the first structure on the site. The right medallion carried the legend "The First Brick Building Erected In Chicago Was Built Upon This Site." Within a year of completion, this was discovered to be untrue, and the right medallion was replaced with one bearing the date "1893," the year construction began.

Behind the doubled entrance doors was the small vestibule spanned by a mosaic vault. Just beyond the vestibule, Sullivan enhanced the entrance hall with marble staircases on either side which met above the vestibule vault and opened to a wide landing on the second (or main) floor before ending at the third floor. The stair balustrades, with Sullivan-ornamented balusters, were of iron, the same material used throughout the building for the grilles enclosing the elevator shafts. On the ground and main floors these grilles were embellished with ornamental cast iron panels and framed by cast iron casings finished in bronze electro-plate. Although few of these grilles survived, the Art Institute was able to purchase one entire bank during demolition from funds generously provided by the Graham Foundation for Advanced Studies in the Fine Arts. A different design, employed for the elevator grilles from floors three through 13, combined strap iron with small iron spheres. Originally given a dark finish, paint, these grilles were ornamented with cast bronze T-plates and, like the ground floor grilles, framed by

bronze-plated cast iron casings. Examples of these assemblies have long been in the Art Institute's collection.

The main staircase to the south on the second floor above the LaSalle Street vestibule. Entrance to Trading Room appears to the right. These stairs were removed in 1908 when the Trading Room was remodeled for the Foreman Brothers' Bank.

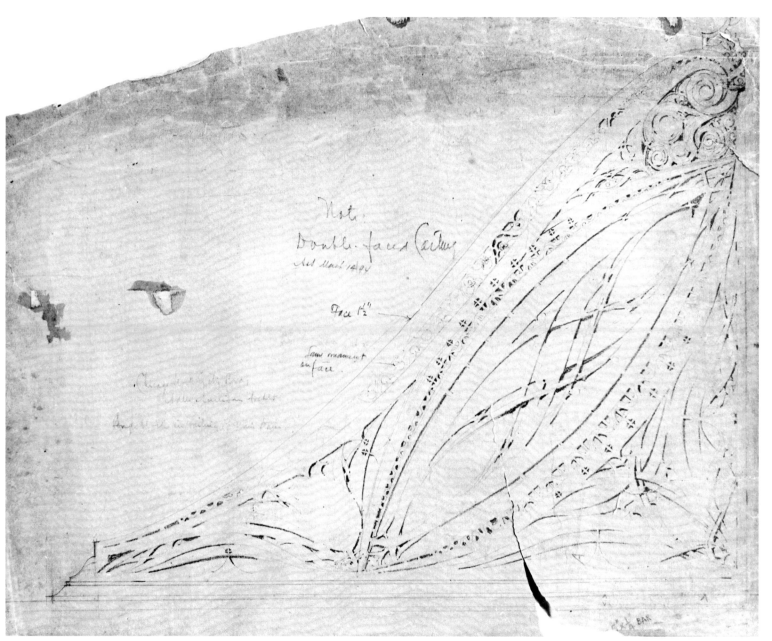

Louis H. Sullivan's drawing for the angle block in the railing of the main stairs outside of the Trading Room.

Elevator grilles used on floors 3-13.

One of the bronze T-plates used on the elevator grilles, floors 3-13.

Photograph taken shortly after the opening of the Trading Room.

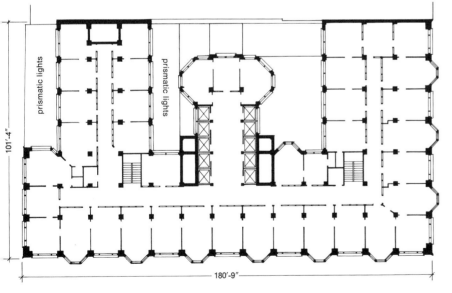

Second (main) floor plan of the Chicago Stock Exchange Building.

Typical floor plan for floors 4-12 of the Chicago Stock Exchange Building.

THE TRADING ROOM

The principal entrance to the Trading Room was on the second floor to the south of the main staircases. Upon entering, the visitor would be unexpectedly confronted by a space with a 30-foot high ceiling, a floor area measuring 64 by 81 feet, and a 16-foot deep gallery running the length of the west wall.

Hailed in its day as "unexcelled in the magnificence of its appointments and decoration by any room used for like purpose in the country," the room was also innovative in its structural design. To fulfill the client's requirement of an unobstructed area for a trading floor, Adler designed a steel framing system which permitted the elimination of intermediate supports, yet carried 11 floors above. A rectangular inverted box of steel trusses above the Trading Room's ceiling transferred the weight of the upper floors to four columns within the room's space. The perimeter of the box was formed by four large trusses, each 13 ft. 6 in. deep. Three additional trusses, each 6 ft. 9 in. deep, bridged its short (40 ft. 6 in.) dimension. A stenciled plaster ceiling, while concealing the trusses, indicated their location and relative depths.

Carbon filament lamps, set in a plaster frieze around the lower inside edge of the inverted box, illuminated the room. The ceiling was of colored art glass, lighted from above by an ingenious system of skylights, whereby natural light filtered through the third floor lunettes in the east and south façades, and through shed roofs of prismatic glass on the north and south. The four monumental columns supporting the trusses were sheathed in scagliola, an artifi-

The Trading Room

Tracing from Adler & Sullivan's drawing
of transverse and longitudinal sections
of the Trading Room.

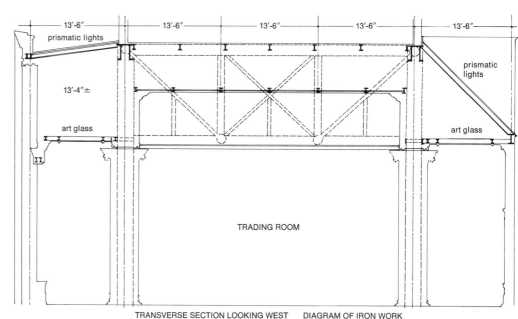

13'-6" 13'-6" 13'-6" 13'-6" 13'-6"

prismatic lights

prismatic lights

13'-4"±

art glass

art glass

TRADING ROOM

TRANSVERSE SECTION LOOKING WEST   DIAGRAM OF IRON WORK

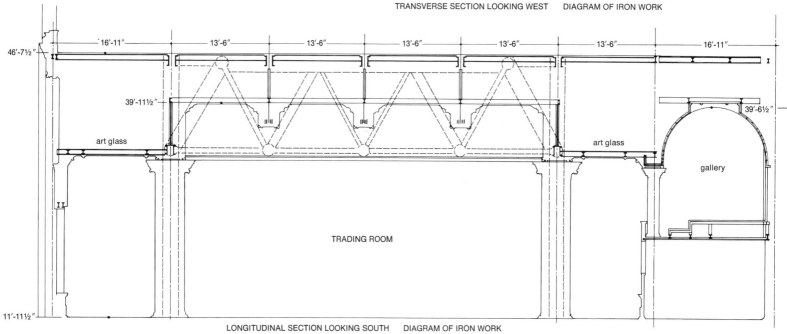

46'-7½"

16'-11"   13'-6"   13'-6"   13'-6"   13'-6"   13'-6"   16'-11"

39'-11½"

39'-6½"

art glass

art glass

gallery

TRADING ROOM

11'-11½"

LONGITUDINAL SECTION LOOKING SOUTH   DIAGRAM OF IRON WORK

cial marble finish, and circled by brass sconces below the gilt plaster capitals.

A striking feature of the room was the contrast between the symmetry of the coffered ceiling and the asymmetry of the interior elevations. Double-hung windows in the east wall overlooked LaSalle Street. Taller windows in the south wall faced an alley separating the Stock Exchange from an adjacent tall structure. The north wall contained the room's entrance and the large slate-boards where trading activities were recorded. Originally, beneath the three-foot diameter clock, stood the panelled and ornamented desk of the Exchange Secretary. The west wall was divided into two stories: the lower level held offices, meeting rooms and toilets as well as telegraph facilities and safes; the visitors' gallery on the upper level was reached by a staircase from the ground floor entrance hall.

The development of the structural daring required to achieve such a space within a skyscraper can be traced to two such earlier Adler & Sullivan projects; the Auditorium Building (1886–90) and the Schiller (later Garrick Theater) Building (1891–92).

The Michigan Avenue lobbies of the hotel incorporated into the Auditorium Building were rectangular spaces on two floors, enclosed in bearing walls, and connected by a grand staircase. Within each space, a line of five cast iron columns sheathed in scagliola supported plaster-encased cast iron beams. Sullivan expressed this traditional post-and-beam construction through the manner in which he orna-

The first floor lobby (left) showing the grand staircase and the second floor lobby (right), known as the Reception Room of the hotel in Adler & Sullivan's Auditorium Building, Chicago.

mented the columns and ceiling, but he wished to interrupt the column spacing to accommodate the staircase, and achieve a dramatic flow of architectural space between the floors. Adler, to meet Sullivan's requirements, designed 33-foot trusses, spanning the stairwell openings on both floors and thereby transferred the weight of the upper floors to piers on either side of the openings.

In the Garrick Theater Building, Adler & Sullivan faced the problem of carrying eight floors of offices above a 1300-seat theater. This space was spanned by huge trusses, 55 ft. long and 22 ft. 11 in. deep, which rested on masonry bearing walls and which carried the structural skeleton of the floors above. From these trusses the semi-circular vaults of the theater shell hung as a thin membrane of plaster.

In the Trading Room, as in the Auditorium Hotel lobbies, the rhythm of the structural system is interrupted to accommodate a dramatic architectural space. As in the Garrick, the plaster membrane of the ceiling is suspended from trusses, but instead of forming an enclosing vault, it is drawn up between the trusses and visually isolated from the surrounding walls by luminous bands of glass so that it seems to float.

Just as certain elements found in the Trading Room can be traced to Sullivan's earlier spaces, so can a further development of its spatial organization and decoration be found in the small Midwestern banks he was to design toward the end of his life.

Proscenium arch in the Garrick Theater, Chicago, by Adler & Sullivan, when it was used as a television studio.

The interior of the National Farmers' Bank, Owatonna, Minnesota, 1907—8, the first of a series of small banks designed by Sullivan for midwest towns in Iowa, Minnesota, Wisconsin, Ohio, and Indiana.

A column capital in the Trading Room gallery prior to demolition.

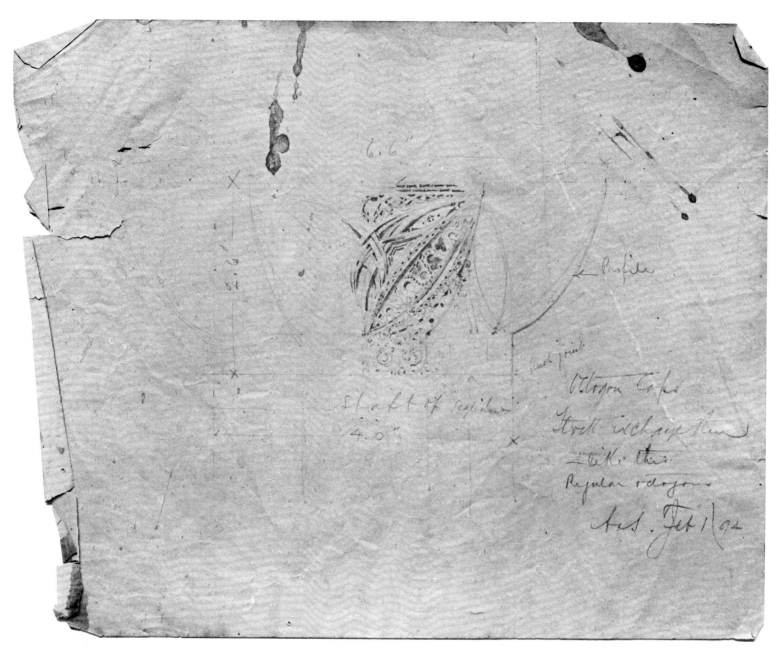

6.6"

Profile

Shaft of capital
4.0"

Octagon Cap.
Stock Exchange Hm
I like this
Regular octagon

Ant. Feb 1/94

Louis H. Sullivan's drawing, dated
February 1, 1894, for one of four main
octagonal capitals in the Trading Room.

Original Trading Room ceiling and one of
the capitals above the false ceiling
which was added in 1940.

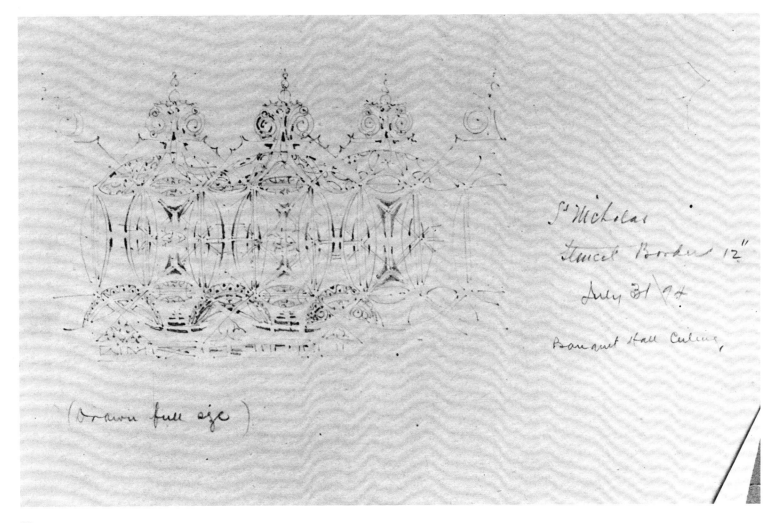

St Nicholas
Stencil Border 12"
July 31 / 94

Banquet Hall Ceiling,

(Drawn full size)

Louis H. Sullivan's drawing for a stencil border in the St. Nicholas Hotel, St. Louis, 1894, now demolished.

Louis H. Sullivan's drawing for stencil, inscribed: "Fresco border/Louis H. Sullivan to John H. Edelman/Paris April 1st 1875."

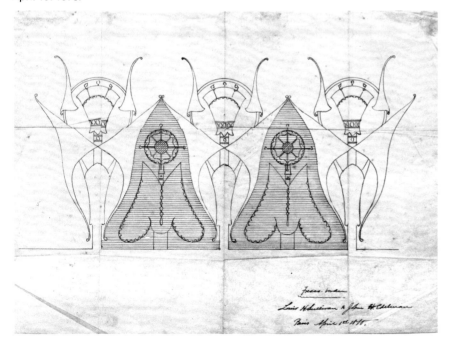

During the nineteenth century, one of the most popular methods of decorating interior surfaces, furniture, and small objects was the ancient technique of stenciling. Voids were cut in a flexible, impervious material, (usually heavy sheets of waxed paper), and paint was forced through the openings with a stiff, short-bristled brush. The technique interested Sullivan; he employed it in his first commissions (the 'frescoing' of the Moody Tabernacle, and the Sinai Temple, both 1876), and developed it to unparalleled richness in the Trading Room.

The commission for the decoration of the new Tabernacle had come to the 20-year-old Sullivan through his friend John Edelmann, whose firm, Johnston & Edelmann, was the building's architect. Sullivan's botanical designs, inspired by his youthful enthusiasm for the writings of botanist Asa Gray, were highly praised in the press. A *Chicago Times* reporter wrote:

The frescoing of the tabernacle is A GRACIOUS RELIEF FROM PAGAN FANTASIES on the one hand, and flagrant abuse and vilification of sentimental devotion on the other. The design is a chaste and elegant architectural conception, wrought out in gorgeous effects of color. The underlying idea is botanical; the anatomy of plants is geometrically treated—the structural growth is carried throughout the forms, and the leaves and the flowers are seen geometrically, that is, without perspective,—as one sees their lines when pressed in the herbarium. The vision is, for an instant, obscure; the design is so recondite and its working-out so scientific that the conception does not become fully apparent until the whole is seen at once, then the unity is obvious and the details reveal themselves in their massive harmony.

But some members of the congregation seemed to hold a different opinion. An interview with the church's founder, Dwight Moody, also appeared in the *Chicago Times*.

"Your church is about ready for occupancy, Brother Moody?"

"Yes, it is looming up finely."

"There seems to be considerable difference of opinion among the congregation as to the character of THE FRES-COING."

"It's a fine job. The artist has done his work well."

"But the principal objection seems to be that it is too 'loud'. What is your opinion?"

"I don't think so. It is peculiar, but I don't see anything out of the way in it. If I had been directing it I might have had something different, but then no doubt just as many would have objected to my style as do to this. Why that work has cost already $2,200 and it would be a shame to throw all that money away. I think the frescoing is in keeping with the rest of the building. This thing of working for and trying to please the public is AN UNGRATEFUL TASK."

The "public" prevailed. By 1882 the stencils had been painted out.

In the design of the Auditorium Building, Sullivan abandoned his earlier polychromatic color schemes and bold botanical forms for the use of elegant gold-leafed arabesques laid over plain grounds. Sullivan described the scheme in a paper published in part in *Industrial Chicago*.

The plaster and color decorations are distinctly architectural in conception. They are everywhere kept subordinate to the general effect of the larger structural masses and sub-divisions, while lending to them the enchantment of soft

A tracing from the original stencils in the Auditorium Theater. Gold on old ivory.

A tracing from the original stencils in the Garrick Theater. Red, green, salmon, gold, and yellow.

tones and of varied light and shade. A single idea or principle is taken as a basis of the color scheme, that is to say, use is made of but one color in each instance, and that color is associated with gold. The color selected varies with each room treated, but the plan of using one color with gold is in no case departed from.

Polychromed stencils of up to five colors were used later in the Schiller (later Garrick) Theater (1891–93). These designs in tones of salmon, green, gold, yellow and red had long been painted over, and were discovered only when the theater was being demolished in 1961. Under the direction of architect Crombie Taylor, the stencil patterns were uncovered and recorded.

The Trading Room stencils, though unsurpassed in their richness and complexity, reflect, in their harmony with the room as a whole, Sullivan's views on the inter-relationship of ornament and structure. In his essay, *Ornament in Architecture* (1892), he wrote:

It must be manifest that an ornamental design will be more beautiful if it seems a part of the surface or substance that receives it than if it looks "stuck on," so to speak. A little observation will lead one to see that in the former case there exists a peculiar sympathy between the ornament and the structure, which is absent in the latter. Both structure and ornament obviously benefit by this sympathy; each enhancing the value of the other. And this, I take it, is the preparatory basis of what may be called an organic system of ornamentation.

The ornament, as a matter of fact, is applied in the same sense of being cut in or cut on, or otherwise done: yet it should appear, when completed, as though by the outworking of some beneficent agency it had come forth from the very substance of the material and was there by the same right that a flower appears amid the leaves of its parent plant.

Sullivan was to use stenciling in his later commissions as well. Noteworthy examples occur in the National Farmers' Bank in Owatonna, Minnesota, (1907–08) and the Home Building Association Bank in Newark, Ohio, (1914). In a letter to his client, Carl K. Bennett, vice president of the National Farmers' Bank, Sullivan confided his fascination in the effects of color. The Millet referred to is his friend Louis J. Millet, who collaborated on the decoration of many of Sullivan's major commissions:

This is to let you know that I arrived right side up and ok; after a 5 o'clock adventure studying the color effects of the lovely grass, of very early skies, as seen along the valley of the Illinois River. My whole Spring is wrapped up just now in the study of color and out of doors for the sake of your bank decorations—which I wish to make out of doors-in-doors if I can. I am not sure that I can, but I am going to try. I am almost abnormally sensitive to color just now and every shade and nuance produces upon me an effect that is orchestral and patently sensitive to all the instruments. I know in my own mind what I am trying to achieve for you and I have in Millet the best chorus master that could be found. I want a color symphony and I am pretty sure I am going to get it. I want something with many shades of the strings and the woodwinds and the brass, and I am pretty sure I am going to get it. There never has been in my entire career such an opportunity for a color tone poem as your bank interior plainly puts before me. It is not half so much a matter as to whether Millet is equal to it as whether I am equal to giving him the sufficiently delicate initiatives. I don't think I can possibly impress upon you how deep a hold this color symphony has taken upon me.

And what I have in mind to accomplish—if accomplish I can. Suffice it to say that Millet is the greatest of colorists extant, and suffice further to say that I am wrapped up in your project to a degree that would be absurd in connection with anyone but yourself . . .

Sullivan was one of the few men in the history of architecture to develop an entire system of ornament in a personal and instantly recognizable style. His accomplishment was acclaimed by his contemporaries, and as the buildings he designed have been destroyed, fragments of his ornament are now artifacts of museum value.

Detail of stencils by Louis H. Sullivan in the National Farmer's Bank, Owatonna, Minnesota.

After the decision was made by the Art Institute to reconstruct the Trading Room, the need became evident for its documentation before the building was demolished. The space had been repeatedly altered and the task of determining its original condition would have to be undertaken before the evidence .was lost.

When the demolition began in 1971, the existence of the great Trading Room had been all but forgotten. Few photographs had been taken of it during the 14 years it had served its original function, and it was ignored by architectural historians. Research indicated that in 1908 the Stock Exchange organization's rent-free lease expired; because of their wish to be nearer to the south end of LaSalle street, they moved to the Rookery Building.

That same year the Foreman Brothers' Bank moved into the Trading Room space. Photographs of the room, as remodeled by the bank, were discovered during the demolition among the archives of the McCormick Estate stored on the Trading Room gallery. These photographs were salvaged before the archives were lost with the demolition of the building. The remodeling muted the original color scheme and blocked the natural illumination of the skylights. In 1929, as the Foreman Brothers' Bank was planning to move into a 38-story building it was erecting across the street, the stock market crashed. The bank failed and the room was abandoned.

The space was not occupied until 1940, when Bell Savings and Loan rented the room. The installation

A main capital and part of the skylight prior to the dismantling of the Trading Room.

of air conditioning required the construction of a suspended acoustical ceiling. The mahogany wainscoting was removed and the floor area subdivided. Ironically, this misuse of the great space protected the ornament in the upper half of the room until the salvage operation began 31 years later.

The final tenant in the space was the U.S.O., which operated a social center for military personnel until the building was vacated.

Demolition had already started before the dismantling of the Trading Room was permitted to begin.

New obstacles presented themselves, but by November 8, 1971, the dismantling process began. Two weeks were required to strip the room of the false ceiling and partitions added in 1940, and to uncover the blocked windows and open up the gallery to the main room. This briefly "restored" the room to its original shape. The Art Institute commissioned Perry Borchers of Ohio State University to make photometric drawings for the Historic American Buildings Survey.

It was discovered that many of the original art glass skylights, though painted or boarded over, were still in place, and that the cast iron mullions which framed them were demountable. More than 400 cast iron skylight mullions, some weighing 175 pounds, were then unbolted, numbered and stored; more than 200 art glass skylight panels were crated and moved to the Art Institute storerooms.

Newspaper descriptions of the Trading Room's opening on April 30, 1894 commented that "No less than 65 colors were used to decorate the room." When the salvage operation began, many of these patterns had long been painted over, so sections were cut from all plaster mouldings, borders and wall surfaces thought to contain such designs. The overpainting was later removed and the patterns recorded. Many of the stencils had been done on canvas, which was peeled from the ceiling and rolled up. The largest such section was taken from the coffered ceiling and measured 7 ft. 8 in. in width by 27 ft. in length.

On January 31, 1972, the last fragments were moved to the Art Institute.

Photographic collage of the Trading Room ceiling before it was dismantled.

Salvaging the Trading Room after the débris and partitions
had been cleaned out.

The Trading Room soon after the false ceiling was removed
to begin the salvaging of ornament.

View looking southeast from gallery in reconstructed room.

Scaffolded room during construction.

A major grant from the Walter E. Heller Foundation through its president, Mrs. Edwin J. DeCosta, made the reconstruction of the Trading Room possible. As the project progressed, escalating costs made it seem that a complete reconstruction would require additional funding, and it was suggested that only a representative portion of the room be rebuilt. Happily, just as bidding occurred, the Walter E. Heller Foundation generously increased its grant and the complete realization of the project was assured. Funds from the Heller grant also made possible reassembly of the Stock Exchange Arch on Monroe Street at Columbus Drive.

The Trading Room was placed within the museum's new east wing, on direct axis with McKinlock Court. Vinci-Kenny, the architects for the reconstruction, urged that the room be placed in its original orientation and provided with natural illumination through skylights and east windows. Since the LaSalle Street site of the building was not in square, the east wall of the Trading Room was 15 inches longer than the west. Skidmore, Owings & Merrill, architects for the Art Institute's new wing accommodated this condition by placing a slightly tapering corridor behind the room's south wall.

On March 31, 1976, the reconstruction began within the concrete block shell. The space was scaffolded and lathers and plasterers began to build up the beamed ceiling which now contains the brilliant stencils. Templates were used to reproduce the heavy plaster moldings, some two inches in radius: an operation done with such skill that tolerances were within a fraction of an inch.

Enough sections had been salvaged of the plaster frieze carrying the initials of the Chicago Stock Exchange to permit installation of entirely original units along the south and west faces of the truss beams. New plaster units were copied for the two remaining sides. Two capitals from the massive octagonal columns existed; these were installed in the southeast and southwest corners. Only fragments of the gallery column capitals had survived, but a typical element was repaired to make the mold from which all four new capitals were cast. Where the original gold leaf of the capitals remained it was retouched; new leaf was applied to the reproductions.

Due to the brittle quality of the scagliola sheathing which had survived on two of the columns, only fragments could be salvaged for use in matching the color and mottling of a new finish. The technique of making scagliola has almost been lost in the United States, but the plaster contractors, after much investigation, located Jay Gould, an artisan in California who understood the process, and who, with his two assistants, was hired to recreate the sheathing of the eight columns.

Ninety-percent of the cast iron mullions supporting the art glass skylights had been salvaged and missing sections were cast in aluminum. Replacing 25 percent of the glass was a difficult project. Colors and textures could not be matched from existing supplies, and glass had to be made to order, which

Plasterers sanding scagliola on a column.

View looking west in the reconstructed room.

View looking east in the reconstructed room.

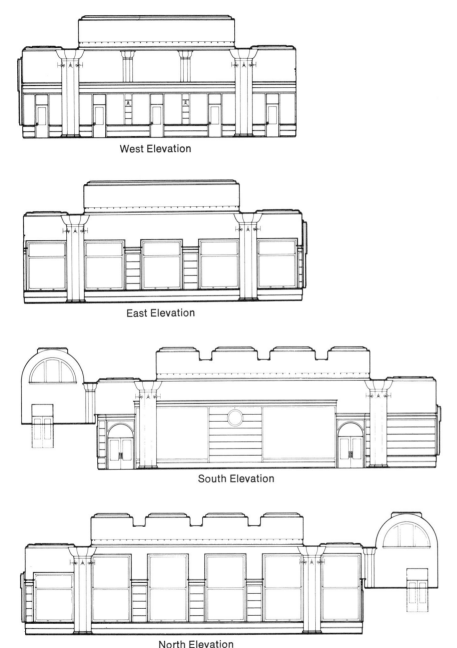

West Elevation

East Elevation

South Elevation

North Elevation

delayed deliveries by as much as a year. The original plaster ventilation grilles had been permanently set into the ceiling. New removable grilles, cast in aluminum, conceal the ducts which now provide both heating and air conditioning in the new room.

The cast iron moldings around the bases of the columns had long been removed, and were redesigned from photographs, then cast in aluminum.

Ductile iron was used for the stair balusters and newel posts, and given the same electroplated finish as the originals.

It was determined that the original hardware had a Bower-Barff finish, a rust-resistant coating commonly specified by Adler & Sullivan. This finish, named for its two developers, was produced by heating the hardware to 1700°F., then injecting steam and volatile hydrocarbon liquids into the furnace to cause the deposit on the metal of a hard, non-porous, gray-black surface. Unfortunately the finish was no longer available, and all new hardware was cast in bronze.

The original window frames and wainscoting were of mahogany. A section of the window frame had been salvaged, but as the wainscoting had been removed 30 years earlier, its placement and detailing had to be painstakingly determined from old photographs. Honduras mahogany was used to replace both frames and wainscoting; red oak was used for the floor.

The richness and complexity of the stencils make them the most impressive single feature of the room.

When the reconstruction project began it was intended to re-use all of the salvaged stencils, and Robert Furhoff was hired to clean and repair them. Missing sections of stencils on canvas, and all stencils that had originally been applied directly to plaster, needed to be reproduced, and Furhoff prepared the drawings and color schedules required. Each of the 15 different stencils had to be broken down into its numerous components and individual colors. An analysis of the stencil used on the interior faces of the main trusses revealed the presence of 52 colors; 31 of these were found, in their original condition, on a three-inch strip of the stencil that had been overlapped during the original installation, and thus protected from light and air.

Furhoff supervised the reproduction of the stencils by working with the painting contractor's staff of stencil cutters and artisans as they interpreted his drawings. Natural rather than synthetic pigments were used in a zinc and oil base, and for ease of installation all the patterns were put on canvas. The results were so satisfactory that it was decided to use original stencil work only in the ceiling bay at the west end of the room.

Tremendous pride of workmanship was exhibited by all trades. The Room quickly took form, and with the exception of the missing art glass, was recreated in 11 months.

Plasterers forming ceiling moldings during the reconstruction.

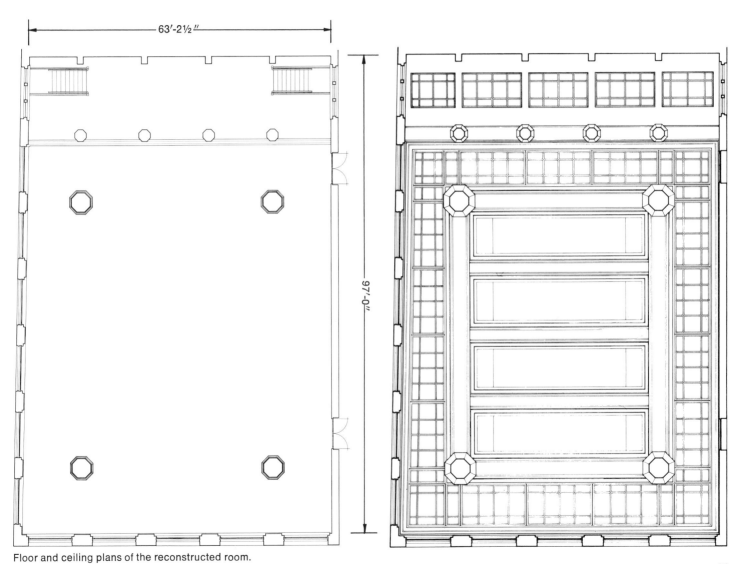

Floor and ceiling plans of the reconstructed room.

Painting wall stencil on canvas.

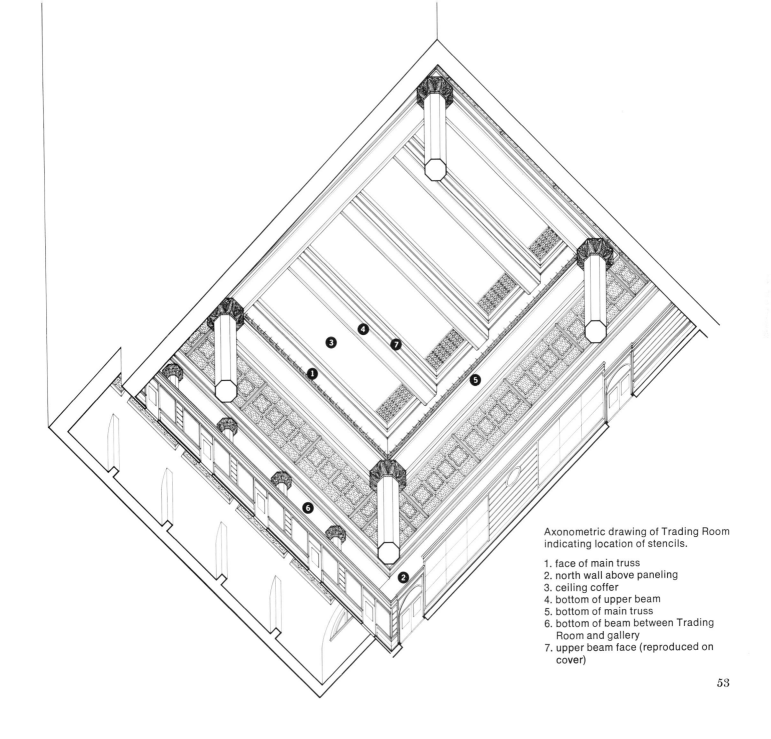

Axonometric drawing of Trading Room
indicating location of stencils.

1. face of main truss
2. north wall above paneling
3. ceiling coffer
4. bottom of upper beam
5. bottom of main truss
6. bottom of beam between Trading
   Room and gallery
7. upper beam face (reproduced on
   cover)

Stencil (1) on the face of the main trusses. 52 colors were applied to the canvas.

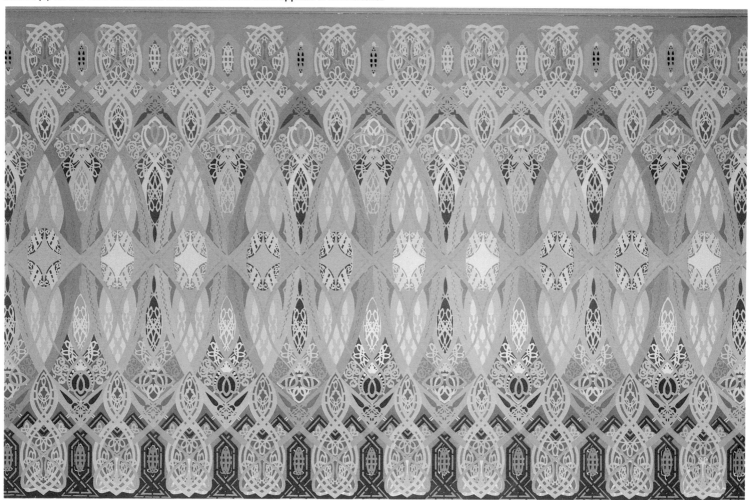

Stencil (2) on the north, east and south walls above paneling. 28 colors applied to canvas.

Ventilating grille in reconstructed room.

Art glass in reconstructed room.

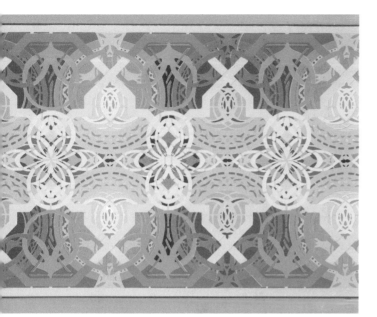

Stencil (4) on the bottom of upper beams. 21 colors applied to canvas.

Stencil (5) on bottom of the main trusses. 24 colors were applied to the canvas.

Stencil (6) on the bottom of beam between the Trading Room and gallery. 8 colors applied to canvas.

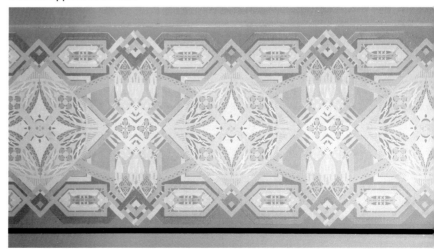

Stencil (3) on the ceiling coffers.
16 colors applied to canvas.

Louis H. Sullivan at 44.

Dankmar Adler at 45.

Dankmar Adler 1844—1900

Dankmar Adler was born on July 3, 1844 in Stadt Lengsfeld, near Eisenach. He came to America with his father, Liebman, in 1854, and they settled in Detroit, where his father became a rabbi and cantor. Dankmar's interest in architectural drawing led his father to apprentice him to an architect in Detroit. In May, 1861, the Adler family moved to Chicago. Ten years later Adler formed a partnership with Edward Burling, but after carrying most of the work load in the partnership, he established an independent practice in 1879. His first project, the Central Music Hall, stood at the corner of Randolph and State Streets until 1901, and was the prototype for a number of theaters he and his partner Louis Sullivan designed in later years. It was Adler's intuitive grasp of acoustic principles that determined the layout of the orchestra, balconies and ceiling coves in these theaters, which included the Auditorium, McVickers, and Garrick Theaters.

Louis H. Sullivan 1856—1924

Louis Sullivan was born in Boston in 1856. His early years were divided between school and his grandparents' farm. He developed a deep respect for the rhythm and structure of nature from the writings of Asa Gray, a botanist and transcendentalist. In 1872 Sullivan entered the architectural school at the Massachusetts Institute of Technology, but left after one year with the intent of studying at the Ecole des Beaux Arts in Paris. Instead, he worked in the office of Frank Furness in Philadelphia, but the panic of 1873 forced him to leave after a short time. Since his parents had moved to Chicago four years prior, Sullivan decided to visit them. Appalled by the ruin left in the wake of the Chicago Fire, yet excited by the prospect of rebuilding, Sullivan took a job as a draftsman with Major William Le Baron Jenny, where he met John Edelmann. Within one year, he left Chicago for the Ecole des Beaux Arts, but returned within a year as draftsman and designer for various firms. In 1880 he worked for Dankmar Adler; their partnership was formed in 1883.

Adler & Sullivan 1881—1895

The firm of Adler & Sullivan executed more than two hundred projects, including over one hundred residences, many stores, warehouses, office buildings, tombs, synagogues, hotels and theaters. Among the most prominent examples of their work in Chicago were the Auditorium Building (1886—90), the Ryerson Tomb (1889), the Getty Tomb (1890), the Schiller Building (later the Garrick Theater Building) (1891—92) the Charnley House (1891), the Transportation Building (1891—93), and the Chicago Stock Exchange Building (1893), and elsewhere the Wainwright Building (1890—92) in St. Louis and the Guaranty Building (1894—95) in Buffalo.

The Chicago Stock Exchange Building was one of the last major buildings designed by Adler & Sullivan before their partnership was dissolved in 1895. The office at that time employed Frank Lloyd Wright and George Grant Elmslie.

ARCHITECTS AND CONTRACTORS

Chicago Stock Exchange Building 1893—1894

Architects: Adler & Sullivan
Civil engineer: William Sooy Smith
Contractor: Victor Falkenau & Brothers
Stained glass and frescoing: Healy & Millet
Masons: Chicago Hydraulic Pressed Brick Company
Ornamental iron: The Winslow Brothers Company
Wood finishing: Brunswick-Balke-Collender Company
Plate glass, mirrors and beveled glass: James H. Rice Company

Prismatic skylights: Brown Brothers Manufacturing Company
Gas and electrical fixtures: Alexander H. Revell & Company
Hardware trimmings: Orr & Lockett Hardware Company
Furniture: J. S. Ford, Johnson & Company
Terra-cotta: The Northwestern Terra Cotta Works of Chicago
Fireproofing: Pioneer Fire Proof Construction Company
Heating and ventilating system: Andrew Johnson Company
Plumbing: T. W. Potts & Company

Reconstruction of the Trading Room and the Stock Exchange Arch 1976—1977

Architects for the reconstruction: Vinci-Kenny, Architects
Structural and mechanical engineers: Skidmore, Owings & Merrill
General contractor for the reconstruction: Reed Illinois Corporation
Painting and decorating: Nelson-Sholin Painting Company
Plastering and lathing: Reed Illinois Corporation
Metalwork: Custom Architectural Metals, Inc.
Millwork: Hartmann-Sanders Company
Art glass: Wenz Art Glass
Glazing: Tyler & Hippach Glass Company
Sconces and clock: New Metal Crafts, Inc.

Marble and Slate: McCue Marble Corporation
Hardware: Clark and Barlow Hardware Company
Floor: Johnson Floor Company, Inc.
Electrical work: Kil-Bar Electric Company
Architects for the Centennial Project: Skidmore, Owings & Merrill,
   Walter A. Netsch, principal in charge of design
General Contractors for the Centennial Project: Morse/Diesel, Inc.
Architects for the reconstruction of the arch: Skidmore, Owings & Merrill
General contractors and masons: Crouch-Walker Corporation
Terra-cotta suppliers: Gladding, McBean & Co.